Unsung

Eric Suddoth

Rising Smoke Publishing

Unless otherwise indicated, Scripture quotations are from:
The Holy Bible, English Standard Version®, ESV©
2011 by Crossway, a publishing ministry of Good News Publishers.
Used by permission. All rights reserved worldwide.

Rising Smoke Publishing
ISBN 978-1-949869-07-1

Oh sing to the Lord a new song;
sing to Lord, all the earth!
Psalm 96:1

Oh sing to the Lord a new song,
for He has done marvelous things!
His right hands and His holy arm
have worked salvation for him.
Psalm 98:1

Praise the Lord!
Sing to the Lord a new song,
His praise in the assembly of the godly!
Psalm 149:1

I have been writing poems and songs for decades, usually in journals or old notepads or on the backs of tattered church bulletins for only my eyes to see. Many of these songs have never been read or heard, unless you were one of the chosen few that I allowed into my circle behind my old upright piano or aged blue guitar, thus the title *Unsung*. However, each of these songs have been sung many times in the quietness of my home where the words and the melodies danced in unison with an audience usually of one, the One. This is a disarming journey, but it is one that I have felt compelled to share. I wanted to release this collection of songs because the majority of these songs started first as prayers, a communion between me and God. As if my words were my fragile offering, as meager as my words may be. Other lyrics arose as a time of worship through the reading of the Holy Word. Each song has a unique story for why it was written and as I have scurried through the countless pages, it is interesting that I still remember the moments I first scribbled these words on any blank space I could find. Some were written many years ago waiting for my next class in the quiet lobby where I should have been studying for my next exam. Some were written after a thought-provoking Bible study with a small group of friends where someone opened my eyes at a once familiar passage. Many were written in the darkened valleys and these became my remnants of hope for myself and my prayers for others. Hope that my journey wasn't fruitless or alone, but that He was with me through the cold and rough terrain. Even when I couldn't see or even imagine the mountaintop, He beckoned me to close my eyes and believe that a peak was within reach. Others were written for no other reason but to show my love to God. I have been blessed by the words that the Lord spoke or sung over me and I didn't want to keep these songs unread. May you find some inspiration through these unheard songs. May you find glimpses of His grace and love throughout the pages. Maybe it will spur you to write your own song to Him. A song that is yearning to be sung.

I am Yours

When I wake refreshed
Let my first breath
Exhale, "Hallelujah"
And when I lie to rest
Let my last breath
Exhale, "Amen"

And may ever breath in between
Be a reminder of your majesty
That the God who gives me air to breathe
Deserves much more than this song I sing

And if this is all I have
I want You to have all of me
Take me, I am Yours
I am Yours

When I am scared to death
Let my next breath
Exhale, "Help me, God"
And when I have nothing left
Let my next breath
Exhale, "I need you, God"

And in times of joy or in moments of pain

Let me be reminded You are still the same

Loving God who stoops down to whisper my name

To tell me that it's going to be okay

And if this is all I have

I want You to have all of me

Take me, I am Yours

I am Yours

And when the sun rises

I will arise for You

And only You

And when the sun sets

I will bow down to You

And only You

Rhythm

Do you hear the heavenly rhythm?
Causing the earth to move
No actions in collision
They're orchestrated by You
By You

So stomp your feet to the ground
Clap your hands and make sounds
Of praise
To His holy name

Do you sense what's becoming?
An army of faithful hearts
No white flags in surrender
We're gonna finish what we start

So lift our hearts to His throne
Fix our eyes on Him alone
My God
Oh, my God

We give praise
We give praise
We give praise
To our God

So stomp our feet to the ground
Clap our hands and make sounds
Of praise
To His holy name

Lift our hearts to His throne
Fix our eyes on Him alone
My God
Oh, my God

Set Eternity in My Heart – *Ecclesiastes 3:11*

Set eternity in my heart
Oh praise, the ancient of days
And forever You will be
Hold me in Your arms
My Redeemer of grace
You love me for me

I want to be with You forever
I want to be with You forever
There is no other place that I want to be
Than with You forever

Set eternity in my heart
Oh praise, the Lord of no beginning
And the God of no end
You love despite my scars
My wounds You're always mending
Like an ever-faithful friend

I want to be with You forever
I want to be with You forever
There is no other place that I want to be
Than with You forever

Heaven is but a breath away
But some days it seems so far
And I cannot wait until the day
When nothing shall keep us apart

I want to be with You forever
I want to be with You forever
There is no other place that I want to be
Than with You forever

Refuge – *Psalm 62*

Two things I have heard
Oh God, You are strong
And You are loving
I will pour out my heart to You
I will trust You to see me through

My soul finds rest in You
My salvation comes from You
You alone are my rock and my salvation
I will not be shaken

You are,
You are my refuge
You are my refuge
My only hope
My only hope

My soul finds rest in You
My salvation comes from You
You alone are my rock and my salvation
I will not be shaken

Mercy

Let the weight of Your mercy
Fall
Fall full on me

Let the weight of Your mercy
Fall
Fall full on me

You alone
You alone
Be exalted

We praise Your name
We lift high Your name

Let the weight of Your mercy
Fall
Fall full on me

King of Heaven

Oh, light of the world
Be the light of my life
Be my love
Be my delight

Oh, ever flowing spring
Be the water I crave
Be my thirst
Be my grace

King of Heaven and earth, You are
King of Heaven and earth, You are
King of Heaven and earth

Great all-powerful God
Holy is Your name
Glorious King
Maker of all my days
Reign with perfect authority on Your throne
I will praise, I will praise You alone
I will praise, I will praise You alone

King of Heaven and earth, You are

King of Heaven and earth, You are

King of Heaven and earth

I will stand before Your throne

I will sing before Your throne

I will dance before Your throne

I will fall

In awe

Of You alone

King of Heaven and earth, You are

King of Heaven and earth, You are

King of Heaven and earth

Feet

I come to You broken
Hoping
You will give me another look

My life's in pieces
Jesus
Please let me just look

At Your feet
Oh, at Your feet

Father, forgive me
Unworthy
I come before You now

At Your feet
Oh, at Your feet

Even though I am honored
To gaze upon Your feet
My heart explodes with excitement
To look up

Into Your eyes
Oh, into Your eyes

Oh, how blessed I am
That You even look at me at all
Oh, how blessed I am
That You look at me with love

My Savior

Suddenly
I see
From a new
Point of view

Instantly
I'm free
From the chains
Bound with shame

And You didn't have to take them away
Yet when I called out Your name
You came
To my rescue

You are my Savior
You are my Savior
When the world passed me by
You stepped into my life
And saved me
You saved me

I'm thankful
Yet unable
To repay
The ransom you paid

Reverently
I'm on my knees
In awe
Of my God

You are my Savior
You are my Savior
When the world passed me by
You stepped into my life
And saved me
You saved me

Wake Up

What's it going to take for us to see
How dependent we are
Yet act so independently
How hard are we going to have to fall
Until we hit the ground
And give You our all

Wake up, wake up, wake up before it's too late
The glory of God is shining brighter than the day
Today, today, today let's praise His name
The past is gone and tomorrow is too far away
To wait

We've seen the history so full of mistakes
You'd think we'd learn
Yet we're following their ways
We live with the belief that it won't happen to us
They thought the same
And look at what they become

Wake up, wake up, wake up before it's too late
The glory of God is shining brighter than the day
Today, today, today let's praise His name
The past is gone and tomorrow is too far away
To wait

If we just turn away from all we hold onto
If we just turn to You
If we just turn to You

If we just throw away all that we cling onto
If we just turn to You
If we just turn to You

Only You

May You hear my heart
Louder than my words
May it be pleasing in Your sight
May my offering of
Praise be of worth
More than gold in Your sight

May my life
Bring you delight
For You are all I live for

And I live for only You
Without You
What would be the use?
I live for only You
Only You

May I bring a smile
Upon Your face
May I be pleasing in Your sight
May I follow
Follow all Your ways
And walk only in Your sight

And I live for only You

Without You

What would be the use?

I live for only You

Only You

You will be

Forever my King

How Can I Say

How can I say
What I really want to say
Without the words getting in the way

How I can do
What I really want to do
Without my actions getting all skewed

How can I be
Who I really want to be
If I don't stop and sit with You quietly

I love
I love you

La La Song

I don't have the words
Even though so many I've heard
Yet none will do its justice
To say how much Your love is

And Your love is
And how You love me is
And Your love for me is

Even still
I don't have the words

La La La La La La La La

Presence

When I close my eyes
The world falls behind
And in an instant
I'm in Your presence

Oh, I am so honored
To be with You now

To know the King of Kings
Is staring right at me
Oh, Lord I am amazed
To be with You in this place

Lord of Heaven, King of earth
Utmost glory and endless worth
Hand of power and loving grace
Defeater of death, the One who saves

Oh, I am so honored
To be with You now

To know the King of Kings

Is staring right at me

Oh, Lord I am amazed

To be with You in this place

Emmanuel

He is here

Here with us

Emmanuel

Great God

God with us

Surrender

What would people say if I raised the white flag?
Walked out on the battlefield, hands chained and gagged
Would they consider me weak?
If I fell at Your feet

Should I revolt against the men that hold me as a slave?
Walk toward Your freedom and never have to look at a grave
Would they consider me weak?
If I fell to my knees

I don't want to live as a slave anymore
I'm surrendering my life without regrets
Walking free to what You have in store
And no matter how many times the sun sets
I will remember
The grace in surrender

I know that this may not always be an easy road
Wandering for forty years may be the way I go
Who cares if I am weak
When I kneel at Your feet

It may have been easier to stay in my chains

To listen to the orders and only have to obey

And if they saw me now

As I lay on the ground

Would they think we weak

As I pray, trembling on my knees

I don't want to live as a slave anymore

I'm surrendering my life without regrets

Walking free to what You have in store

And no matter how many times the sun sets

I will remember

The grace in surrender

And the road of pride is paved in cement

When the road I travel is of only sand

And even though my path might change with the wind

At least the Kingdom of God will be closer at hand

I will remember

The grace in surrender

Holy

They stood by and watched in awe
With the power You displayed in Your hands
And when You
Created the blue
Sky that stretched over the horizon
Their knees were weak and they couldn't stand

They kneeled by and stared at Your wonder
They shook at the sound of Your thunder
And when the green
Divided the sea
And land appeared before their eyes
They could not contain their joy inside

Holy, Holy, Holy is the Lord
Holy is the Almighty God

They watched Him with brush in hand
As He stroked beauty across the land
And the trees
Sprouted their leaves
And the flowers covered the landscape
They knew these colors would never wash away

They stared as He molded lumps of clay
There must have been millions displayed
And the statues
Began to move
And they let out their powerful roars
And then humbly knelt before the Lord

Holy, Holy, Holy is the Lord
Holy is the Almighty God

In just six days
All of this was made
But He still had one more thing to create

They watched Him begin to smile
As He breathed into a lifeless pile
Of dirt
From the earth
And suddenly a heavenly transformation
Caused this dirt to be a living creation

And a man in God's own image kneeled
And the angels were stilled

Holy, Holy, Holy is the Lord
Holy is the Almighty God

But Not Anymore

I've lost some feeling
But I can still touch
The hardness of leather
That used to comfort me so much
But not anymore

I've lost some hearing
But I can still listen
The stillness in the void
That used to be loud and shaken
But not anymore

Somehow I've lost a part of me
That knew a part of You
But I don't even know where or when I let it go
I just know
I let it go

I lost some vision
But I can still see
The beauty that eclipsed
Is now a memory

It's gotten away

Away from me

It's gotten away

Away from me

But I want it back

A Little Grace

How can You give so freely?
Even when You see all we try to hide
You don't harbor any grudges
Yet I can't forget the words they said that one night

And I don't want to forgive them
No, I don't want to forgive them

But who am I to say
They don't deserve forgiveness
And who am I to choose
To whom to be a witness
And it is so hard sometimes to have faith
When I can't even show a little grace

How can I believe a concept?
When I only want it to pertain to my side
Wouldn't my faith be useless
If all of God's perfect planning turned on a dime

And would You then want to forgive me?
Would You want to forgive me?

But who am I to say
They don't deserve forgiveness
And who am I to choose
To whom to be a witness
And it is so hard sometimes to have faith
When I can't even show a little grace

Everyone should feel the freedom of mercy
Everyone should experience redemption
Everyone deserves a lifetime to feel worthy
Everyone deserves a chance for salvation

And why is it so hard
When You give it so freely?

And it is so hard for me to believe in grace
But it might be easier to have faith
If I learned to give a little grace

Tremble

My Savior defeated what's never lost before
He conquered the sleep with just one breath, my Lord
And the earth shook with a fight
And Your grave exploded with life
My Savior defeated what's never lost before

And I tremble at the thought
I tremble at the thought
That Jesus Christ
Died for my life
And I tremble
I tremble at the thought

You were thinking of me long before time began
Before I knew You, You had a plan
And the God that held the seas
With the same hands crafted me
You were thinking of me long before time began

And I tremble at the thought

I tremble at the thought

That Yahweh

He knows my name

And I tremble

I tremble at the thought

Absence from this body means presence with the Lord

Even though I'm not ready, each day I get a little more

So I will live by faith

Waiting for the day

When absence from this body means presence with the Lord

And I tremble at the thought

I tremble at the thought

When I will see

My God, my King

And I tremble

I tremble at the thought

Maps and Globes

I said a prayer
To take me where
I've never been before
And You took me to my own backyard
But it looked different, it felt strange
I saw something more

I've traveled the lands
Dreamed of distant sands
Yet it was here all along

I heard crying
The tears were trying
To console themselves
A single mom, who's lived next door for years
She looked different, and I felt scared
Yet I knew I could help

I've traveled the lands
Dreamed of distant sands
Yet it was here all along

How many years
Have I missed out?
Dreaming or trying
To figure out
How to get there
How to get there

How many maps
Have I thrown darts at?
Hoping that it
Would start a path
To get there
To get there

No more globes to spin
No more wandering
I am here
Gonna spread my roots
Until they intertwine with You
I'm going to get there
Cuz I am here

Family Tree

It appears it was a tornado
That split their tree in two
It was once grand and strong
But now it's showing its roots
The leaves have all departed
The limbs are now bare
They have scattered alone
And now none of them care

Tornado, please, do not pass over our tree
It is newly planted and starting to sprout its first leaves
The roots are not that strong
It could be easily swayed
So, please Tornado, do not hit our tree today

It appears it was a fire
That scorched their tree to ash
It was once tall and beautiful
But now its nothing to look at
No one knows what caused the spark
Looks like someone threw gas on the fire
And when someone threw some water
It only intensified the flames desire

Fire, please, do not set our tree ablaze

We are watering it so it will be strong one day

The limbs are very fragile

The leaves easy to ignite

So, please Fire, do not scorch our tree tonight

It appears it was a snowstorm

That sheeted the tree with ice

It was once lovely and enticing

Now its frozen and breaking without a vice

No one did anything to save the tree

There was not enough warmth to survive

And the tree never recouped after the storm

It seems like it just gave up and died

Ice, please, do not coat our tree limbs down

They are very weak and it would just weigh them down

The tree would easily

Break to the hard ground

So, please Ice, do not weigh our tree down

And we have weathered these occasions in our first year

Our family tree will survive

It will my dear

So Be It

This is to all you naysayers
Who say it cannot be done
This is to all you dream haters
Who gave up before you ever begun

You who never see the victory in all your history of battles
You only see a life of dreams and other mysteries as a hassle

So be it
So be it
But that's not the way I see it
And you can dwell
On the empty well
That has run dry
But there's another one overflowing
Somewhere only hoping
To be found
But you'll never reach it
Sitting down
So be it

This is for all the critics

Who only live to rustle up feathers

This is for all the cynics

Who never see things as getting better

You will never see an answered prayer since you never ask

You only see a life of obstacles as impossible to pass

So be it

So be it

But that's not the way I see it

And you can dwell

On the empty well

That has run dry

But there's another one overflowing

Somewhere only hoping

To be found

But you'll never reach it

Sitting down

So be it

Commit to the Lord whatever you do,

And your plans will succeed

These may be scoffed at by man,

But not the God who speaks in dreams

We Can

It is the weak that will move the mountains
It is the poor that will feed the hungry
It is the cripple that will lead the march for the thousands
It is the orphan that will comfort the lonely

We can, we will
The earth will be stilled
To their knees
When they see
That we can and we will

It only takes one dream to become a vision
And only one vision to form a plan
And that plan can evolve into a mission
And that mission can revolutionize this land

We can, we will
The earth will be stilled
To their knees
When they see
That we can and we will

So use us for Your glory
Use us for Your glory

You're Still God

If it be sunshine or pouring rain
In a time of healing or a period of pain
You're still God

Whether the cold of winter or the life of spring
To be given plenty or to behold nothing
You're still God

In the stillness of peace or the chaos of war
To see dreams come to pass or a closing of a door
You're still God

To embrace the morning dawn or to toss at midnight
To wrestle with my doubts or to walk along insight
You're still God

You're God even when life is hard
You're God when life is a work of art
You're God from one day to the next
You're still God when we take our last breath

You're still God

Footprints

Oh, it's been such a long journey
Many obstacles I have crossed
But despite the twisted path
I never once got lost

I can see the footprints of the saints
Who have gone before
And if I close my eyes I can see them by myside
Along with the Lord's

Help me Lord to keep this pace
To keep my faith
To keep this pace
To finish the race

Many times, I have felt awed
Knowing that millions have been here
And through their faith
I know I too can persevere

And it's so sad to see the footprints of those
That have drifted off the path
But it just fans the flames for me,
Because I don't want to go out, go out like that

Help me Lord to keep this pace

To keep my faith

To keep this pace

To finish the race

And I can see the footprints of the saints

Who have gone before

And it makes me wonder will the next generation

See mine, mine beside Yours

He Loves You

Close your eyes
And rest in the arms who love you
Let it go
And give it up to the One who will carry it for you
Who wants this heavy burden
Who wants to continue hurting
When there is someone who is willing to take it for you

And He stands upon a hill
On a cross to reveal
How much He loves you
How much He loves you
And if He endured all the pain for you then
Don't you think He'll take it away again
So you don't have it feel it
Cuz He's still willing

Lay it down
And just walk away and He will hold onto it for you
Toss aside
All that hinders you from living a life you want to
Who wants to live unhappily
When someone is willing to carry
All your doubts and fears and He is begging to take them for you

And He stands upon a hill

On a cross to reveal

How much He loves you

How much He loves you

And if He endured all the pain for you then

Don't you think He'll take it away again

So you don't have it feel it

Cuz He's still willing

No matter your struggles

He's man enough to take them

Don't worry about your battles

He's warrior enough to slay them

Don't fret about your fears

He's big enough to outweigh them

And He will

He will

In Memoriam

Some days, your light was the only one they saw

When so many candles flicker, yours remained strong

And it wasn't always an easy road you traveled on

But so many people found their paths cuz you carried on

Well done, well done my child

Watch as the world stands still for you

Gaze upon their lives and smile

For you touched each one with your love

So well done my child, well done

I've crafted beauty in My hands for anyone to see

Carving out the canyons or swirling the galaxies

But no matter how much I mold the greatest sight will be

Photographs of your grace-filled life will be My masterpiece

Well done, well done my child

Watch as the world stands still for you

Gaze upon their lives and smile

For you touched each one with your love

So well done my child, well done

And all who knew you got to know Me
And all who saw you got a portrait of Me
And all who heard you got a word from Me
For you were always My hands and feet
You were always My hands and feet

Well done, well done my child
Watch as the world stands still for you
Gaze upon their lives and smile
For you touched each one with your love
So well done my child, well done

When – Heal My Scars

You cause the waves, You hold the stars
With the same hands that heal my scars
You hold it all
From great to small
And not even a grain of sand
Can ever slip through Your hands

Yet when I fall
Why do You let me fall
When You can catch me
Safely in Your palms
And when I hurt
Why do You let me hurt
When You could have stopped it
Before it occurred
But yet You let me hurt

With just Your finger You drew the line
Causing a boundary between the ground and sky
And how did it feel
When light revealed
What Your hands had made
And Your glory is still displayed

Yet when I fall
Why do You let me fall
When You can catch me
Safely in Your palms
And when I hurt
Why do You let me hurt
When You could have stopped it
Before it occurred
But yet You let me hurt

And You were God who carved out the mountains
And You are big enough to know where the universe ends
And even though
I know You still love me just as much as way back when
I can't help but question

When I fall
And when I hurt
Why do You let me hurt
When You could have stopped it
Before it occurred
But yet
You let me hurt

But yet
You cause the waves, You hold the stars
With the same hands that always heal my scars

49

Fall Back

When You whisper
My heart does not race anymore
You're familiar
And each day seems like the one before
Will You wake me up from my slumber
Show me something to look at in wonder
Because I want to
Fall back in love with You

Make my knees weak
So I'll have to kneel at Your throne
Jog back my memory
Of times when I was Yours and Yours alone
And sitting at Your feet
Was the best place to be
So help me love You
Like how I used to

I caught a glimpse
Of a smile in my own reflection
And I asked if this
Was caused by You to get my attention
I felt a joy that mere words could not explain
Nothing funny happened, I just felt a change
And in an instant I knew
I was falling back to You

Make my knees weak
So I'll have to kneel at Your throne
Jog back my memory
Of times when I was Yours and Yours alone
And sitting at Your feet
Was the best place to be
So help me love You
Like how I used to

Next time you whisper
I hope my heart races a little more

Without Limit

My error of sin
Oh Lord, You have seen
But through Your love
I live redeemed
My jaded past
Caused more than scars
But through Your wounds
You mended my heart

And I wonder, with how much I've done to cause You shame
When will I ever use up the last remains of Your grace
But You say

My grace is without limit
There will never be a day
When My love will fade
It's without limit

You knew my past
Before I was born
You know what's to come
Long before me Lord
And yet You died
To spare me pain
Even though You knew
I'd wear the sinners stains

And I wonder, if You ever wanted to back out of the cross
When You thought that my sins were not worth such a cost

My grace is without limit
There will never be a day
When My love will fade
It's without limit

To the liars, the whores, the scoundrels and the thieves
The murderers, the rapist, the drunkards, the druggies
The hypocrites, the atheists, the addicted and the weak
He did not pick and choose which sins His blood would clean

Oh, His love is limitless
Nothing is as endless
As the east is from the west
It is limitless

These Storms

With my arms spread wide
I can feel the heavens sprinkle
And as the storm comes alive
It may cause tears and wrinkles

But I will still hold my hands high
Raising them to the angry sky
Singing

They don't control my life
Storms will come and pass
They don't make me hide
I will stand as long as they last
And even though You formed these storms
I can trust You to be my Lord

My strength is fleeting
One hand is still raised
The other one is keeping
A firm grip to Your name

And I will try to hold my hands high
Raising them to the angry sky
Singing

They don't control my life

Storms will come and pass

They don't make me hide

I will stand as long as they last

And even though You formed these storms

I can trust You to be my Lord

Cry out to Me in your storms

Cry out, I will hear

Cry out to Me in your pain

And I will sustain you

They don't control my life

Storms will come and pass

They don't make me hide

I will stand as long as they last

And even though You formed these storms

I can trust You to be my Lord

Formed

He could have been a normal man
Claiming to be someone He was not
For a chance to make history took a stand
With a proclamation as the Son of God
Knowing He would have some followers and some enemies
Who would cause a scene for what they believed
Even one that would cause Him to die
What a better way to be remembered by
Those left behind

But my faith wasn't formed in His death
No, my faith wasn't formed in His death

Some could say He was not in sound mind
Gathering with the sinners and the outcast
What joy could a holy man even find
In the company of those who were always thought of last
Maybe He knew in confusion would heighten more questions
When He said in three days there would be a resurrection
But first He would have to give up His life and die
What a better way to be remembered by
Those left behind

But my faith wasn't formed in His death
No, my faith wasn't formed in His death

But could a normal man raise to life after three days?
And could a crazy man call angels down to His grave?
And could a lying man have the power of God to proclaim?

With wounds on His hands
And a hole in His side
He was once a dead man
But now He is alive

But my faith wasn't formed in His death
No, my faith is formed in His life
My faith is formed in His life
My faith is formed in His life
Because anyone can die
But only He came back to life

Blessed

Poor little girl, doesn't know how bad she has it
This is her world, so she doesn't even try to mask it
She doesn't know any better
She works in the fields in all kinds of weather
But she doesn't complain
When it droughts or when it rains

Yet she smiles
And considers herself blessed
Because she has somewhere to live
And a quiet place to rest
And it may not be the best
But through the eyes of a child
She sees she is blessed

Fragile little boy, doesn't know what lies ahead
Since he was his momma's joy he's laid in his bed
He doesn't know any better
Sometimes his cancer makes him as weak as a feather
But he doesn't complain
When all he feels is the pain

Yet he smiles

And considers himself blessed

Because he has someone to love him

With every one of his breathes

And his life may not be the best

But through the eyes of a child

He sees he is blessed

And she may never know the feeling of four sturdy walls

And he may never know the excitement of hitting a baseball

But miracles always come when you search for awhile

Usually they are only seen through the eyes of a child

And here I am in my new car and my suit is pressed

And I feel the weight of the world and all the stress

But my life is better

Than I give it credit for

Yet I seem to always complain

When things don't work out my way

Blessed are you

And you will receive

The Kingdom of Heaven

Thoughts

Everyone tells me to be quiet
Questions only show your doubt
So I left the stones unturned
And started walking aimlessly around

Where am I going?
What am I showing
In this life?
In my confused life

And the thoughts that I was thinking,
I was thinking,
I was the only one thinking them
And it shocks me to know
I'm not alone

The dust has settled over my belongings
Leaving an inch of covering
I trace my finger along the filth
And notice that I am discovering

A new clean layer
And my finger didn't make the surface grayer
It didn't make it any grayer

And the thoughts that I was thinking,

I was thinking,

I was the only one thinking them

And it shocks me to know

I'm not alone

I've worried too long about offending tradition

For twenty years I've recited their rendition

Following man's rules led me astray to a new expedition

On how to find You, yet I'm left with a mission

To find You for myself

And the thoughts that I was thinking,

You might have been thinking them

The same time I was thinking them

And isn't it nice to know

We're not alone

Remain in My Love – *John 15:7*

The world seems to be growing colder
And it's so easy to just walk away
But please, come, come a little closer
And let Me whisper words you want Me to say

I'll never let you go
If you always stay
I'll always grab ahold
If you
Remain
In My love

Leaving is to simple a path to choose
I go one way and you go the other
Both ways, you and I both lose
Cuz I'll miss you more than you could discover

I'll never let you go
If you always stay
I'll always grab ahold
If you
Remain
In My love

Crows – *Peter's Denial*

One never thinks they are capable of
The darkest schemes they can think up
And before you know it, here it comes
At full force
With no choice

A snowball never slows its roll down
And a domino never holds its own ground
They each fall victim to the system of now
In a blink
You're at your brink

Quicksand often resembles cement paths
It only takes one step to cause an avalanche
Or regretful turn arounds of aftermaths
Think you're fast
Now you're last

In the distance
Can you hear it?
A rooster crows

Different – *Inspired by Walking on Water: Reflections on Faith and Art by Madeleine L'Engle*

I want to be different
I want to be different
It's taken awhile for me to come to terms with that fact
I don't want to be common
Don't want to be common
Like everyone else standing beside me walking the same path

Because if we were all the same
My light would not be shined by Your flame

I want You to make me
Into a living mystery
And the only explanation I could give for my life
Would be You

I used to want to follow
Used to want to follow
But I fell into too many pits being led by the blind
It took a rock and a hard place
A rock and a hard place
To finally open my eyes to see what I was to find

Because if I just followed the crowed

My light would have been snuffed out

I want You to make me

Into a living mystery

And the only explanation I could give for my life

Would be You

And I want my life to be

A witness for all to see

That my life would not make sense

If You did not exist

In the Meantime – *Abraham and Sarah*

One would think
It would be second nature by now
Waiting for the day
When everything would be worked out

But days still pass
But the passing still isn't easy
When you think at last
Today will be a new beginning

Oh, to know the happy endings before they come
Would it lose its awe?
If I knew it all
I don't cross my fingers waiting for the rising sun
Because I know
It's going to show

But if You don't want to show me a sign
Please hold my hand
In the meantime

Will there come a day

That my heart will tell me to walk away

To sweep up my faith

Move on with the broken pieces that remain

But what if I gave up one day too soon

When each day is planned

Like the lines on my hand

What if giving up, meant giving up on You

When any obstacle

Is always possible

But if You don't want to show me a sign

Please hold my hand

In the meantime

Give me faith

To know

To give up or wait

In hope

But if You don't want to show me a sign

Please hold my hand

In the meantime

The Day After

Did this really happen?
I've pinched myself till I bruised
I see the hill
Where He was killed
But it still doesn't seem to be true

We were just laughing
What seems like the other night
As I look back
I should have
Seen the dotted lines that ended His life

Now here we are
To scared to breathe
Huddled in the dark
Holding onto memories

I watched Him raise the dead
So why hasn't He yet?

What now do I do?

For three years I followed Him

It's only been

A day shut in

Where do I start again?

Now here we are

To scared to breathe

Huddled in the dark

Holding onto memories

I watched Him perform many signs

Or was I just blind?

I guess I should have listened

To the doubters I tried to convince

Because they are not hiding

Or hoping for some providence

But something is telling me to hold on

Pitfalls

If you asked me then
How I have been
I would have said a clever alright
But life is filled
With rolling hills
That cause us to stumble and to climb

Because once you think you've made it
You just made
A big mistake

Because towering walls
Can't guard against pitfalls
That are inevitably sure to come
No matter how hard you try
Someone waits nearby
To take your place when you're done
Or even when you're not done

We all try to keep
Wounds buried deep
So that no one can touch the scars
We shovel on the dirt
Even though it hurts
In hopes that the pain forgets our heart

Because when you think you've created
A safe place to hide
The world comes to fight

Because towering walls
Can't guard against pitfalls
That are inevitably sure to come
No matter how hard you try
Someone waits nearby
To take your place when you're done
Or even when you're not done

So I will hold onto
The One that holds onto me
And I will see
You were always holding me

Because when you think you've stated
All there is to say
Silence backs away

Proven

Love,
You carried their hate
So I could embrace
Your love, Your awesome love
Nailed like a thief
On Calvary's tree
Just to prove, prove Your love

But have I proven my love?
When have I proven my love?
Why have I not proven my love
To You?

Oh Jesus,
Savior of my soul
Please don't let me go
Cuz, I love You
Oh, how I love You

Let these words
Be a start to prove
How much I love You
Cuz, I love You
Oh, how I love You

Love,
Your love gives me hope
But have I ever showed
Your love, Your awesome love
To someone in need
Desperate or hurting
Just to prove, prove Your love

But have I proven my love?
When have I proven my love?
Why have I not proven my love
To You?

Oh Jesus,
Savior of my soul
Please don't let me go
Cuz, I love You
Oh, how I love You

Let these words
Be a start to prove
How much I love You
Cuz, I love You
Oh, how I love You

Cuz words only go so far

And words only do so much

When a broken heart

Sometimes needs just a touch

We are, we are

Your hands to give love to the loveless

We are, we are

Your feet to go out to the hopeless

We are, we are

Your eyes to see the beauty in the worthless

Cuz You did it for us

You did it for us

Take Me Away

This is the time to take a stand
No more waiting around for a strong hand
To do something we are called to do
Follow You

This is the reason we were made
To rise up and make a difference today
To do something that may be brand new
Follow You

For You will not leave us
Or even lead us
In the wrong direction

So Holy Spirit take me away
Take me away
To where You want me to go
I will follow
Take me away, take me away
I don't need to know
To follow
For you are God
And I am not
So take me away

No matter what comes our way
You are faithful, You will not go away
You'll give us strength to continue
To follow You

For You will not desert us
Or even force us
In Your direction

So Holy Spirit take me away
Take me away
To where You want me to go
I will follow
Take me away, take me away
I don't need to know
To follow
For you are God
And I am not
So take me away

In a world that's broken

You can fix it all

You can heal it all

It's not that I am boasting

Cuz I can't fix it all

No, I can't heal at all

No, You're the reason for my hoping

My God can fix it all

My God can heal it all

You just want us to come along

So, take us to the sick and the dying

To the weary and the crying

To the wounded and degraded

To the slaved and the hated

To the hungry and the homeless

To the depressed and the hopeless

To the widows and the orphans

To the natives and the foreign

To our neighbors and family

To the forgotten over seas

To the prisoners and the users

To the abused and the abusers

Take us away

Take us away

God, take us away

Because – *1 John 4:19*

Because You came as the son of man

Because You lived so we could understand

Because You died for our transgressions

But mostly because

You're alive again

You're alive again

Jesus, we will praise Your name

Shout it out, we're not ashamed

We want the world to hear

We want the world to know

Jesus, we will lift Your name higher

We'll shine a light, ignite a fire

We want the world to see

We want the world to know

That the reason You love us

Is just because

Because You still break every chain

That holds us down in guilt and shame

Because You make us new everyday

But mostly because

You know my name

You know my name

Jesus, we will praise Your name
Shout it out, we're not ashamed
We want the world to hear
We want the world to know
Jesus, we will lift Your name higher
We'll shine a light, ignite a fire
We want the world to see
We want the world to know
That the reason You love us
Is just because

Because You first loved us
We love You because You first loved us
We love You because You first loved us

Drifting

Let the sea roar
I'm not afraid
Anymore

Let the tides rage
I'm no longer
Afraid

And I may be sinking
But at least I'm sinking into You
And I may be drifting
Let me drift beside You

Cuz You are my Prince of peace
You are the only One I need
You are always faithful
Even when I'm not able
To see
You are
You are with me

Let the storm come
I know You're
Not done

Let the winds blow

I know I'm

Not alone

And I may be sinking

But at least I'm sinking into You

And I may be drifting

Let me drift beside You

Cuz You are my Prince of peace

You are the only One I need

You are always faithful

Even when I'm not able

To see

You are

You are with me

Cannot – *Jeremiah 20:9 and Romans 1:20*

The heavens declare the works of Your hands
Your glory's displayed all over this land
How can I overlook Your splendor?
How can I not surrender
To praise Your name?

There's a fire raging in my bones
If I don't praise Your name
It's bound to lose control

And I cannot keep it in
I cannot, I cannot
I cannot keep it in
I cannot, I cannot

Your invisible qualities are forever seen
Your divine nature knows no boundaries
I am without an excuse
How can I not choose
To praise Your name?

There's a fire raging in my bones
If I don't praise Your name
It's bound to lose control

And I cannot keep it in

I cannot, I cannot

I cannot keep it in

I cannot, I cannot

As the fire grows

Let me give You praise

As the fire grows

Let me praise Your name

And I cannot keep it in

I cannot, I cannot

I will not keep it in

I will not, I will not

I will not

I am Coming

If I called You
Would You even come?
If I fell to my knees
Would You even see me
Or just the mess I've become?

If I cried out
Would You even come?
If I unsilenced the night
Would You even fight
Your way to my battlefront?

Will You come?

I am coming!
I am coming!
No grave or cross
Could ever separate us
I am coming!
I'm on my way!

If I stepped up
Would You even come?
If I took a leap of faith
Would You come to save the day
Or is there something better to be done?

Will You come?

I am coming!
I am coming!
No grave or cross
Could ever separate us
I am coming!
I'm on my way!

I am coming for you
I will always come for you
I even know your past
Your lies and secret masks
I'm on My way
There's nothing you could do
To make Me stop loving you

I am coming for you!

Midst of Thorns

Oh, mount Calvary
The very hill that set me free
Where You bled
Of crimson red
Like the color of a rose
But they didn't
They didn't know

And the story goes
That You were the Lord
You were the rose
Caught in the midst of the thorns

It was only
Three nails to kill the holy
Helpless You cried
Blameless You died
Whiter than snow
But they didn't
They didn't know

And the story goes
That You were the Lord
You were the rose
Caught in the midst of the thorns

Weaved into a crown
Thistles pressed into Your brow
Pain stricken, blood sprinkled
Yet Your eyes had a twinkle
Of everlasting hope
That they didn't
They didn't know

And the story goes
That You were the Lord
You were the rose
Caught in the midst of the thorns

And my story goes
That You are my Lord
You were the rose
Caught in the midst of my thorns

Who Would Have Thought?

With just two fish and some bread
The hungry were fed
Till their bellies were full and their eyes were opened
For faith always surpasses our hopes
Like when the baskets of leftovers overflowed
To show God can take our crumbs and feed the broken

Who would have thought?
That the fish he caught
Would feed the thousands
Would feed the thousands

Righteous wasn't something that she claimed
She didn't have anything to her name
Except for a penny compared to the elite
But a humble heart showed much more
Than the expensive robes he wore
And sadly his pride will never make him complete

Who would have thought?
That her penny meant a lot
More than his thousands
More than his thousands

His fish fed the thousands
When it was broke in His hands
Her offering was better than
The gift from the proud man
But what does this have to do with me?

He wore a crown, but not of gold
His glory was foretold
Yet few faithfully followed Him
Dying in agony was the price He paid
To wash all our sins away
Just so we wouldn't be condemned

Who would have thought?
That my God
Would die for the thousands
Would die for the thousands

Who would have thought?
That my God
Would die for me
He would die just for me

Cling

Is life supposed to be like this?
Did You really plan it out this way?
When everything I try to hit, I always miss
And I just want to look forward to the next day

And why is life sometimes so hard?
When nothing seems to fit into place
I struggle, I claw to watch my guard
And I just end up on my wounded face

And I know You won't let me down
When everything falls through my hands
You cling to me with a plan
And I feel You are always around
To pick me up every time I fall
I know You are there when I need You most of all

Am I on a journey, a lonely traveler,
Wounded and homeless and all alone?
Yet some may see me as just a scavenger
I'm searching for a place to call my own

And I know You won't let me down

When everything falls through my hands

You cling to me with a plan

And I feel You are always around

To pick me up every time I fall

I know You are there when I need You most of all

And I now realize

That when I had tears in my eyes

I could not fully see

The lessons You were teaching me

And I know You haven't let me down

When everything fell through my hands

You clung to me with a plan

And I felt You were always around

You picked me up every time I fell

Even when I thought hope couldn't prevail

And I know I never walked alone

Through the deserted, shadowed valleys

You were always in front of me

And I know You were leading me home

Through all the trials that were resolved

You were with me

You were with me

You were with me through them all

By Your Wounds – *Isaiah 53:5*

My scars are mine and mine alone
I grip the blade and cut in deep
I've been hit by more than words and stone
Each one has caused my flesh to bleed

I have to do this on my own
There's nothing that can bind my heart and soul
There's no string long enough
To stitch me, stick me back up

By Your wounds
I am healed?
How can it be?
Who are You
To be killed
To heal me?

Sadness comes in the darkness nights
And lingers till my strength gives way
I hide the proof that I'm not alright
But if they saw it, what would they say?

There's got to be more to life than just yesterday

Than partaking in this sweater masquerade

I want to move on and come clean

But I put on, put on my long sleeves

By Your wounds

I am healed?

How can it be?

Who are You

To be killed

To heal me?

Oh, the pain isn't felt anymore

Oh, the pain isn't felt anymore

I just want to feel something real

I just want to know how it feels

To be healed

Miles

I tiptoe my fingers
Across a globe
And stop to a place I've never been
In their photographs
I see their lost hope
Reflections of what could have been

Why did You place me here?
And them out there?
Oh, the miles that stands between us
And if our roles were reversed
Would they even care
That there were miles in between us?

I can discard
Their sorrowful eyes
But I cannot forget what I've seen
It's so overwhelming
To hear families cry
For help from the injustice of slavery

Why did You place me here?

And them out there?

Oh, the miles that stands between us

And if our roles were reversed

Would they even care

That there were miles in between us?

Your mercy, my God

Has been shown to me

It's now, my time

To show them the same mercy

Why do You give us an abundance?

Then leave their pockets empty?

Oh, the wealth that stands between us

And if our lives were reversed

Would they give up their luxury

To save my life?

To save my life?

Would they save my life?

How can I not try to save theirs?

Once Again – *Micah 7:18-20*

Once again You have compassion on me
You trample my sins and cast them into the sea

You delight in showing me Your love
You love to show me Your love

Oh God, there is no one else like You
There is nothing that can equal
Not one that can come close
Oh God, who else can do what You do?
There is nothing that can replace
Not one that can come close
You are the One and Only

Once again you pardon me from the sins I've done
You paid my ransom by trading in Your son

Through Your pain You were showing Your love
You took the pain just so I could have Your love

Oh God, there is no one else like You

There is nothing that can equal

Not one that can come close

Oh God, who else can do what You do?

There is nothing that can replace

Not one that can come close

You are the One and Only

You're more faithful than I deserve

With unfailing love, well beyond my worth

You're more faithful than I deserve

With unfailing love, far beyond my worth

We Just Hope

Weeks have gone by
But not as many as we would like
But we live in the past with every day
And we try to hold on
I guess it's true what they say
That life must go on

We cannot live for the past
We cannot dream about what's ahead
We need to live like this day is our last
But we never do
We just hope for the future instead

I lit a candle what feels like the other day
The flame has been out for a month
I'm trying to shine the light, show the way
But the melted wax is not enough
And I guess it's true what they say
It all comes down to faith

We cannot live for the past

We cannot dream about what's ahead

We need to live like this day is our last

But we never do

We just hope for the future instead

And it is good to hope

But hoping never saves any lives

And it is good to dream

But dreaming never opens the blind man's eyes

And I guess it's true what they say

That before you can claim defeat

You have to at least

Try

Palms

Doubt appears to be easier
Than fully relying on You
Holding onto a grain of sand
Is sometimes like holding the truth
Cuz it can slip between my fingers
But it's always caught in Your hands

I'm letting go of everything
I'm placing my life in Your palms
I'm releasing all my insecurities
And I'm watching the worries fall
Into Your palms

Tying strings on my worries
Was my plan to retrieve them
But when I pulled on the thread
I never did receive them
Cuz when I placed it in Your hands
You said You'll never let go

I'm letting go of everything
I'm placing my life in Your palms
I'm releasing all my insecurities
And I'm watching the worries fall
Into Your palms

You held my burdens
Even when I was hurting
And You never gave them back to me

And if I looked at Your hands
Where the nails went through
There I would find my worries
Right beside Your wounds

And I'm letting go of everything
I'm placing my life in Your palms
I'm releasing all my insecurities
And I'm watching the worries fall
Into Your palms

Dead

I remember vividly when You whispered in my ear

Told me all the hurdles I will clear

And I have seen Your outstretched hand

Leading me to where I now stand

But now I see a towering wall

And You tell me that it's going to fall

But I fear I'm not strong enough anymore

But it's never been about my abilities

And I don't hold the countless galaxies

And I can't comprehend

What You'll do in the end

All I know is what You said

And Your promises don't go dead

Days, weeks, months, even years have gone by

The bricks and mortar are mocking my cry

Can you tell me when these rocks will tumble?

Because my faith is already starting to crumble

And all I see is this growing wall

And I can't hear You say anything at all

And I hear I'm not good enough anymore

But it's never been about my abilities
And I don't hold the countless galaxies
And I can't comprehend
What You'll do in the end
All I know is what You said
And Your promises don't go dead

And You're the God of big dreams
Yes, You are the dreamer of possibilities
And with You and the dream You gave
I have what I need, You'll make a way

And all things are possible with You
Yes, all things are possible with You
And I can't comprehend
What You'll do in the end
All I know is what You said
And Your promises don't go dead

All Things – *Philippians 4:13*

It's not that I'm ashamed to be a nerd
It's just that I am more than what you observe
And I can do things that would blow your mind
But it's not me, I got to tell you this time

I can do all things through Christ who gives me strength
I can do all things through Christ who gives me strength

Look at yourself, tell me, what do you see?
A person that you always wanted to be
But in case you are far from your lifetime goal
I have a secret of immense hope

You can do all things through Christ who gives you strength
You can do all things through Christ who gives you strength

Take a look at people with success
Do you think they were always the best
Even if they take all the glory for themselves
Sorry to rain on their parade, but I got to tell

You can do nothing on your own but
We can do all things through Christ who gives us strength
We can do all things through Christ who gives us strength

Only You Know What You Said

You're not as distant as we make You out to be
For You are closer than the honeysuckle air I breathe
And You are sweeter,
So much sweeter

You're not as silent as we believe You are
For You speak more often than the beat of my heart
If we just listen,
We would hear You

You are not as invisible as some have proclaimed
For Your fingerprints can be found on everything
And You have signed it
With Your love

And we think that this is all about us
Yes, we think it all revolves around us
But we didn't speak
The sun to greet
Its first day
No Lord, only You know what You said
So please, keep on saying it

Pray

It's more than a motto
It's not just a verse
It's grander than a cluster
Of a few choice words
And it is more
So much more

When we pray
What can stand in our way
Because in Jesus name
We pray

Our lands can be healed
Our relationships mended
The hungry could be fed
Wars can be ended
And many more
So much more

When we pray
What can stand in our way
Because in Jesus name
We pray

We pray

With believing authority

With pure authenticity

With complete humility

And when we pray

What more can we say

Than in Jesus name

In Jesus name

We pray

Let Your Light Shine Upon Us – *Psalm 4*

Oh my God, please hear my prayer
Be merciful to me
Set me apart, from the rest of the world
Oh Lord, let them see

Let Your light shine upon us
Let Your light shine upon us
Let Your light shine upon us

Oh my God, You have filled my heart
With joy too great to keep in
No matter where I go, I'm going to show it
For Your grace has no end

Let Your light shine upon us
Let Your light shine upon us
Let Your light shine upon us

In the darkest nights
When they're chained in fears
Shine Your light, shine

When all hope is gone
When it has disappeared
Shine Your light, shine

When everything has left them
Except for their tears
Shine Your light, shine

Shine, shine, shine

Let Your light shine upon us
Let Your light shine upon us
Let Your light shine upon us

Shiver

Looking back there have been times
When I lost my fear of You
That the God who holds the mountains up
Can let them fall and I would too

I don't shiver when I see Your wonder
I don't fumble my words in a stutter
And I don't even lose my breath at the sound of Your thunder
Anymore

I cannot recount a very small list
When I sat in awe of Your power
That the God who guides the stars at night
Can let them fall this very hour

I don't shiver when I see Your wonder
I don't fumble my words in a stutter
And I don't even lose my breath at the sound of Your thunder
Anymore

You could let all Hell break loose
You could let the sturdy crumble
You could allow the certain to collapse
You could dissolve the pride to fumble

I don't shiver when I see Your wonder

I don't fumble my words in a stutter

And I don't even lose my breath at the sound of Your thunder

Anymore

I've lost my fear

But I don't feel like

But I don't feel like

I lost anything I wanted

See the Smoke?

Do you see the smoke?
See the smoke that's burning?
Do you see the smoke?
See the smoke that's burning?

Is there any visible proof of my passion?
Or am I but words with no actions?
I feel a fire raging deep in my bones
And I want to know,
Do you see the smoke?

Do you see the smoke?
See the smoke that's burning?
Do you see the smoke?
See the smoke that's burning?

Wherever I walk am I blazing a path?
When I look back, do I leave remnants of ash?
Oh, I feel heat as if stirring the coals
And I want to know,
Do you see the smoke?

Do you see the smoke?
See the smoke that's burning?
Do you see the smoke?
See the smoke that's burning?

And if I feel the burn
But no one sees the flame
Will they know?
How would they know?

And if I continue to burn
And I scream Your name
When I am alone
How will they know?

I can't keep this in my bones
It's got to come out
It's got to come out

I hope they see the smoke
See the smoke that's burning
I hope they see the smoke
See the smoke that's burning
For You

Still / Steal

But I hold onto Your perfect timing
As I watch the days go by
When my friends clouds silver lining
Forms into a tornado in my life

And I can run
Or I can hide
Or I can kneel in the hardest times

Still my beating heart
Still my beating heart

When everyone is finding their treasures
Mine is still hidden in the deserts sands
And Lord, help me not to measure
My worth in the dollars of man

And I can be rich
Or I can be poor
But either way, all I long is to be Yours

Still my beating heart
Still my beating heart

Take me, take me,

Take all of me

Make me, make me,

Make me who I am to be

You are, You are all that I need

So steal me, steal me,

Go on and steal me

And when the crowds begin to stare

Confused at the joy in my laugh

When they point out my despair

Help me to hold onto Your rod and staff

Because You love me

You love me

You want me,

You want me

So steal my beating heart

So steal my beating heart

Coffee for Two

I smell the aroma from the kitchen
I've been itchin'
For a cup
To wake me up
I picked up the paper and I read the news
It only gave me the blues
To read
About the tragedies

I hear the last drip and let out a breath
I take a hot sip and look to my left

And we begin to converse
About the days getting worse
And how things need to be getting better
So I changed the subject to the weather

I stir my drink not to let the sugar settle

To the bottom of the kettle

Sometimes the depth

Holds the best

And I pose questions of moral dilemma

As I let my cup simma'

To burn

Is a lesson learned

And we begin to communicate

And it turns into a debate

Because I sometimes cannot understand

Your reasoning on this man

I fix another cup and offer one to You

But You're through

Two cups of coffee

Too much caffeine

I look to my watch and I notice the time

A quarter till nine

I dump my drink

In the kitchen sink

And we end our dialogue

I say farewell, so long

Let's make plans to do this again

Coffee for two

Just me and You

Amen

If you have enjoyed *Unsung,* check out Eric Suddoth's other books.

 A well-reviewed murder mystery.
https://www.amazon.com/gp/product/1949869008/ref=dbs_a_def_r
wt_bibl_vppi_i0

Solomon's Dreams – The Hunting at Huntington

Solomon "Solo" Davis is a man of faith, but even for him not all things are believable. How quickly his life is turned upside when he comes face to face with one of his doubts. Can he believe in something that is so impossible?

What if your dreams of last night…

"Top story tonight," read the senior news anchor. Solo held his breath, waiting to hear about the kidnapping or the death of the older couple. He had already had two of his dreams strangely come true with frightening detail, and he couldn't help but wonder if it was some cosmic coincidence; a million to one chance that all his dreams actually occurred. Could this really be happening?

Became your reality for today?

"Oh God! Oh God! Oh God! What do I do? What do I do? What do I do?" Solo prayed hoping the perfect answer would drop out of the sky at his feet. The thought sickened him that if his dream with the preschool students with their laughter and singing was real. Then the ruthless kidnappers and serial killers must be real. And the crying, terror stricken kidnapped girl must be real too.

How can you do nothing when you know something is going to happen?

Watch out Washington D.C. The Carbon Monoxide Killers are on the loose.

"Are you ready for this?" she asked her father who slowly nodded, taking in a deep breath.

"It's now or never."

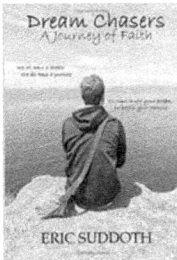

https://www.amazon.com/gp/product/1949869059/ref=dbs_a_def_r
wt_bibl_vppi_i1

Dream Chasers – A Journey of Faith

We all have a dream. We all have a purpose. It's time to use your dream to fulfill your purpose. We were created to dream, but so often we lose the childlike innocence of dreaming of things to come. This book is a compelling reminder that God has an incredible purpose for everyone's life. The Bible is filled with stories of people following their dreams – walking to freedom through a sea, defeating giants with mere pebbles, or watching loved ones be healed. These people dreamed big dreams, but not from their own imagination or merit. No, God ordained these great men and women of faith to chase their dreams, just as He still does today. In this captivating book, mystery and inspirational author, Eric Suddoth engages dreamers to begin a journey they were destined to walk. First steps are always scary, but we are on this journey together. It's time to be Dream Chasers.

"From the stories to the scriptures to the lessons offered and advice given, this book offers waterfall after waterfall of Godly inspiration. The ink on the paper dances in optimism. In casual, easy to read form this book offers readers deep truths anchored in God's word. You will walk away refreshed and ready for whatever comes next." John R. Wallace, author of soon to be released *Chasing Beauty*.